Cat Poems

Cat Poems

edited by Tynan Kogane

A New Directions Paperbook

This book is dedicated to Holly, Chaloupe, Kitty, Tiny, Mochi, Tiger, Tiffany, Pumpkin, Pumpernickel, Sweet Potato (aka Spuds), Donny, Earl, Cosette, and all the other cats we have known and loved.

Manufactured in the United States of America
New Directions Books are printed on acid-free paper
First published as a New Directions Paperbook in 2018
Design by Marian Bantjes

Library of Congress Cataloging-in-Publication Data
Names: Kogane, Tynan, 1985– editor.
Title: Cat poems / edited by Tynan Kogane.
Description: New York : New Directions, 2018.
Identifiers: LCCN 2017051738 | ISBN 9780811227506
(acid-free paper)
Subjects: LCSH: Cats—Poetry.
Classification: LCC PN6110.C3 C36 2018 |
DDC 808.81/93629752—dc23
LC record available at https://lccn.loc.gov/2017051738

10 9 8 7 6 5 4 3 2 1

New Directions Books are published for James Laughlin
by New Directions Publishing Corporation
80 Eighth Avenue, New York 10011

Table of Contents

WILLIAM CARLOS WILLIAMS	9	Poem
DENISE LEVERTOV	10	The Cat as Cat
CHARLES BAUDELAIRE	11	Cats (LXIX)
AMY LOWELL	12	To Winky
STEVIE SMITH	16	My Cat Major
RYSZARD KRYNICKI	17	Frail Manuscripts
GAVIN EWART	18	Sonnet: Cat Logic
KENNETH REXROTH	19	Cat
JAMES LAUGHLIN	20	The Kenner's Cat
STEVIE SMITH	21	The Hound Puss
JAMES TATE	22	The Flying Petunias
EMILY DICKINSON	24	She Sights a Bird
CHARLES BAUDELAIRE	25	The Cat (LIV)
ROBERT DUNCAN	28	A Little Language
FERNANDO PESSOA	31	Magnificat
WILLIAM CARLOS WILLIAMS	32	The Cats' Month
ELIZABETH BISHOP	33	Lullaby for the Cat
ELIOT WEINBERGER	34	"On a cold, rainy, February night"
STEVIE SMITH	35	Friskers
EDWARD LEAR	36	The Owl and the Pussy-Cat
LOUIS ZUKOFSKY	38	Third Movement: In Cat Minor

EZRA POUND	39	Tame Cat
CHARLES BAUDELAIRE	40	The Cat (XXXVI)
PATRIZIA CAVALLI	41	"You want me to be like one of your cats"
LAWRENCE FERLINGHETTI	42	The Cat
WILLIAM CARLOS WILLIAMS	44	The Young Cat and the Chrysanthemums
RAINER MARIA RILKE	45	Black Cat
MURIEL SPARK	46	Bluebell Among the Sables
EUGENIO MONTALE	48	On a Stray Cat
STEVIE SMITH	49	The Galloping Cat
CHRISTOPHER SMART	52	from *Jubilate Agno*
ROBERTO BOLAÑO	58	"No one sends you letters now"
JAMES LAUGHLIN	59	You Know How a Cat
KAWAI CHIGETSU-NI	60	Propriety
JEAN JOUBERT	61	Ancient Cat
EZRA POUND	62	"Mediterranean March"
AMY LOWELL	63	from "Chopin"
STEVIE SMITH	64	Cat Asks Mouse Out
FRANZ KAFKA	65	Little Fable
DENISE LEVERTOV	66	The Innocent

BASIL BUNTING	67	from "The Pious Cat"
JUNG TZU	69	My Dressing Mirror Is a Humpbacked Cat
EDWIN BROCK	70	Hurry Up Please Its Time
KIM HYESOON	73	I'll Call Those Things My Cats
W. B. YEATS	76	The Cat and the Moon
HANS FAVEREY	78	"The muffled thud with which the strange cat"
WILLIAM CARLOS WILLIAMS	79	Mujer
ROBERT SOUTHEY	80	To a College Cat
KAZUKO SHIRAISHI	82	Seven Happy Cats
WILLIAM COWPER	84	from "The Retired Cat"
JOSÉ GARCIA VILLA	85	"A,cat,having,attained, ninehood,"
NICANOR PARRA	86	Pussykatten
THOMAS GRAY	88	Ode on the Death of a Favourite Cat . . .
STEVIE SMITH	91	My Cats
GUILLAUME APOLLINAIRE	92	The Cat
Sources	93	

Poem

As the cat
climbed over
the top of

the jamcloset
first the right
forefoot

carefully
then the hind
stepped down

into the pit of
the empty
flowerpot

DENISE LEVERTOV

The Cat as Cat

The cat on my bosom
sleeping and purring
—fur-petalled chrysanthemum,
squirrel-killer—

is a metaphor only if I
force him to be one,
looking too long in his pale, fond,
dilating, contracting eyes

that reject mirrors, refuse
to observe what bides
stockstill. Likewise

flex and reflex of claws
gently pricking through sweater to skin
gently sustains their own tune,
not mine. I-Thou, cat, I-Thou.

CHARLES BAUDELAIRE

Cats (LXIX)

Feverish lovers, scholars in their lofts,
Both come in their due time to love the cat;
Gentle but powerful, king of the parlor mat,
Lazy, like them, and sensitive to draughts.

Your cat, now, linked to learning and to love,
Exhibits a taste for silences and gloom—
Would make a splendid messenger for doom
If his fierce pride would condescend to serve.

Lost in his day-dream, he assumes the pose
Of sphinxes in the desert, languidly
Fixed in a reverie that has no end.

His loins are lit with the fires of alchemy,
And bits of gold, small as the finest sand,
Fleck, here and there, the mystery of his eyes.

(translated from the French by Anthony Hecht)

AMY LOWELL

To Winky

Cat,
Cat,
What are you?
Son, through a thousand generations, of the black
    leopards
Padding among the sprigs of young bamboo;
Descendant of many removals from the white
    panthers
Who crouch by night under the loquat-trees?
You crouch under the orange begonias,
And your eyes are green
With the violence of murder,
Or half-closed and stealthy
Like your sheathed claws.
Slowly, slowly,
You rise and stretch
In a glossiness of beautiful curves,
Of muscles fluctuating under black, glazed hair.

Cat,
You are a strange creature.
You sit on your haunches
And yawn,
But when you leap
I can almost hear the whine
Of a released string,
And I look to see its flaccid shaking
In the place whence you sprang.

You carry your tail as a banner,
Slowly it passes my chair,
But when I look for you, you are on the table
Moving easily among the most delicate porcelains.
Your food is a matter of importance
And you are insistent on having
Your wants attended to,
And yet you will eat a bird and its feathers
Apparently without injury.

In the night, I hear you crying,
But if I try to find you
There are only the shadows of rhododendron leaves
Brushing the ground.
When you come in out of the rain,
All wet and with your tail full of burrs,
You fawn upon me in coils and subtleties;
But once you are dry
You leave me with a gesture of inconceivable
    impudence,
Conveyed by the vanishing quirk of your tail
As you slide through the open door.

You walk as a king scorning his subjects;
You flirt with me as a concubine in robes of silk.

Cat,
I am afraid of your poisonous beauty,
I have seen you torturing a mouse.
Yet when you lie purring in my lap
I forget everything but how soft you are,
And it is only when I feel your claws open upon my
    hand
That I remember—
Remember a puma lying out on a branch above my
    head
Years ago.

Shall I choke you, Cat,
Or kiss you?
Really I do not know.

STEVIE SMITH

My Cat Major

Major is a fine cat
What is he at?
He hunts birds in the hydrangea
And in the tree
Major was ever a ranger
He ranges where no one can see.

Sometimes he goes up to the attic
With a hooped back
His paws hit the iron rungs
Of the ladder in a quick kick
How can this be done?
It is a knack.

Oh Major is a fine cat
He walks cleverly
And what is he at, my fine cat?
No one can see.

Frail Manuscripts

The old poet's frail manuscripts
bear traces of ash, countless cigarette
holes, coffee stains, less often,
red wine, and now and then
the almost unintelligible prints
of cat paws, vanishing

into spacetime.

(translated from the Polish by Clare Cavanagh)

GAVIN EWART

Sonnet: Cat Logic

Cat sentimentality is a human thing. Cats
are indifferent, their minds can't comprehend
the concept 'I shall die', they just go on living.
Death is more foreign to their thought than
to us the idea of a lime-green lobster. That's
why holding these warm containers of purring fur
is poignant, that they just don't *know*.
Life is in them, like the brandy in the bottle.

One morning a cat wakes up, and doesn't feel
disposed to eat or wash or walk. It doesn't panic
or scream: 'My last hour has come!' It
simply fades. Cats never go grey at the edges
Like us, they don't even look old. Peter Pans,
insouciant. No wonder people identify with cats.

Cat

There are too many poems
About cats. Beware of cat
Lovers, they have a hidden
Frustration somewhere and will
Stick you with it if they can.

JAMES LAUGHLIN

The Kenner's Cat

on whom I sat went by the
name of Jasper and Bucky

Fuller also sat upon said
cat but isn't there more

to it than that   a cat who
holds his place against a

man must surely once have
been back in another life

a man of strongest will &
mind   who was he then invincible

Genghis Khan or
bloodsoaked Attila was he

Arjuna or the elephantine
Hannibal   was he El Bert-

rans sower of discord or
was he just another cat?

The Hound Puss

I have a cat: I call him Pumpkin,
A great fat furry purry lumpkin.
Hi-dee-diddle
hi-diddle
dumpkin.
He sleeps within my bed at night,
His eyes are Mephistopheles-bright:
I dare not look upon their blight.
He stalks me like my angry God,
His gaze is like a fiery rod:
He dines exclusively on cod.
Avaunt, you creeping saviour-devil,
Away with thy angelical evil!

The Flying Petunias

When I let the cat in I didn't see
that it had a mouse in its mouth. But then
it set the mouse down on the kitchen floor
and they proceeded to play cat and mouse.
How very apt, I thought. The mouse stood about
one foot from the cat and the cat would extend
one leg slowly and touch the mouse on its head.
The mouse would sort of bow in supplication.
Then the mouse would dash on and snuggle up
under the cat's belly. One time the mouse
ran up the cat's back and sat on the crook
of her neck, and the cat seemed calmly proud
to have it there. They kept me entertained
like this for about an hour, but then it
started to irritate me that they had this
all worked out so well and I threw the cat
out. The mouse ran under the kitchen sink.
I let kitty in when it was our bedtime.
She has her pillow and I have mine and we've
always slept very sweetly together. In the
middle of this night, however, I feel these
tiny feet creeping across my neck and onto
my chin. I open my eyes slowly and kitty

is staring at me from her pillow and I am staring at her. Then I close my eyes and she closes hers and we all three dream of joining the circus.

EMILY DICKINSON

She Sights a Bird

She sights a Bird—she chuckles—
She flattens—then she crawls—
She runs without the look of feet—
Her eyes increase to Balls—

Her Jaws stir—twitching—hungry—
Her Teeth can hardly stand—
She leaps, but Robin leaped the first—
Ah, Pussy, of the Sand,

The Hopes so juicy ripening—
You almost bathed your Tongue—
When Bliss disclosed a hundred Toes—
And fled with every one—

CHARLES BAUDELAIRE

The Cat (LIV)

I

A fine strong gentle cat is prowling
As if his bedroom, in my brain;
So soft his voice, so smooth its strain,
That you can scarcely hear him miowling.

But should he venture to complain
Or scold, the voice is rich and deep:
And thus he manages to keep
The charm of his untroubled reign.

This voice, which seems to pearl and filter
Through my soul's inmost shady nook,
Fills me with poems, like a book,
And fortifies me, like a philtre.

His voice can cure the direst pain
And it contains the rarest raptures.
The deepest meanings, which it captures,
It needs no language to explain.

There is no bow that can so sweep
That perfect instrument, my heart:
Or make more sumptuous music start
From its most vibrant cord and deep,

Than can the voice of this strange elf,
This cat, bewitching and seraphic
Subtly harmonious in his traffic
With all things else, and with himself.

II

So sweet a perfume seems to swim
Out of his fur both brown and bright,
I nearly was embalmed one night
From (only once) caressing him.

Familiar Lar of where I stay,
He rules, presides, inspires and teaches
All things to which his empire reaches.
Perhaps he is a god, or fay.

When to a cherished cat my gaze
Is magnet-drawn and then returns
Back to itself, it there discerns,
With strange excitement and amaze,

Deep down in my own self, the rays
Of living opals, torch-like gleams
And pallid fire of eyes, it seems,
That fixedly return my gaze.

(translated from the French by Roy Campbell)

ROBERT DUNCAN

A Little Language

I know a little language of my cat, though Dante
     says
that animals have no need of speech and Nature
abhors the superfluous.   My cat is fluent.   He
converses when he wants with me.   To speak

is natural.   And whales and wolves I've heard
in choral soundings of the sea and air
know harmony and have an eloquence that stirs
my mind and heart—they touch the soul.   Here

Dante's religion that would set Man apart
damns the effluence of our life from us
to build therein its powerhouse.

It's in his animal communication Man is
     true, immediate, and
in immediacy,   Man is all animal.

His senses quicken in the thick of the symphony,
     old circuits of animal rapture and alarm,
attentions and arousals in which an identity
     rearrives.

He hears
particular voices among
the concert,   the slightest
rustle in the undertones,
        rehearsing a nervous aptitude
yet to prove *his*.   He sees the flick
        of significant red within the rushing mass
of ruddy wilderness and catches the glow
        of a green shirt
to delite him in a glowing field of green
        —it *speaks* to him—
and in the arc of the spectrum color
        speaks to color.
The rainbow articulates
        a promise he remembers
he but imitates
        in noises that he makes,

this speech in every sense
the world surrounding him.
He picks up on the fugitive tang of mace
        amidst the savory mass,
and taste in evolution is an everlasting key.
        There is a pun of scents in what makes sense.

Myrrh it may have been,
the odor of the announcement that filld the house.

He wakes from deepest sleep

upon a distant signal and waits

as if crouching, springs

to life.

FERNANDO PESSOA

Magnificat

When will this inner night—the universe—end
And I—my soul—have my day?
When will I wake up from being awake?
I don't know. The sun shines on high
And cannot be looked at.
The stars coldly blink
And cannot be counted.
The heart beats aloofly
And cannot be heard.
When will this drama without theater
—Or this theater without drama—end
So that I can go home?
Where? How? When?
O cat staring at me with eyes of life, Who lurks in
        your
depths?
It's Him! It's him!
Like Joshua he'll order the sun to stop, and I'll wake
        up,
And it will be day.
Smile, my soul, in your slumber!
Smile, my soul: it will be day!

(translated from the Portuguese by Margaret Jull Costa)

The Cats' Month

Your frosty hands
your withered face
the merciless February
of it all—
It is for cats!
Their musk
clings in the entries
to good ladies' houses.
I catch it sometimes
even in the open street
where deep snow lies.

ELIZABETH BISHOP

Lullaby for the Cat

Minnow, go to sleep and dream,
    Close your great big eyes;
Round your bed Events prepare
    The pleasantest surprise.

Darling Minnow, drop that frown,
    Just cooperate,
Not a kitten shall be drowned
    In the Marxist State.

Joy and Love will both be yours,
    Minnow, don't be glum.
Happy days are coming soon—
    Sleep, and let them come...

ELIOT WEINBERGER

On a cold, rainy, February night in New York, I remembered the story André Malraux used to tell—and which, at some remove, was told to me—about Mallarmé's cat, whose name, almost needless to say, was Blanche.

On a cold, rainy, February night in Paris, a thin and bedraggled alley cat, wandering the streets, looks in the window of Mallarmé's house and sees a white, fat, and fluffy cat dozing in an overstuffed chair by a blazing fire. He taps on the window:

"Comrade cat, how can you live in luxury and sleep so peacefully when your brothers are out here in the streets starving?"

"Have no fear, comrade," Blanche replied, "I'm only pretending to be Mallarmé's cat."

STEVIE SMITH

Friskers
or
Gods and Men

Oh what can be happening pray what are they at?
Oh why am I slowly turning into a cat?
Is it Zeus responsible, tired of my love
Does he send me outside with the puss cats to
      rove?
Or indifferent rather, quite sick of it all,
Is he simply letting Hera have her way with a rival?
Oh look at my beautiful coat and my handsome
      whiskers,
I shall be most loved of all the young cats and I shall
      be called
Friskers.

EDWARD LEAR

The Owl and the Pussy-Cat

The Owl and the Pussy-cat went to sea
  In a beautiful pea-green boat,
They took some honey, and plenty of money,
  Wrapped up in a five-pound note.
The Owl looked up to the stars above,
  And sang to a small guitar,
"O lovely Pussy! O Pussy, my love,
  What a beautiful Pussy you are,
    You are,
    You are!
What a beautiful Pussy you are!"

Pussy said to the Owl, "You elegant fowl!
  How charmingly sweet you sing!
O let us be married! too long we have tarried:
  But what shall we do for a ring?"
They sailed away, for a year and a day,
  To the land where the Bong-Tree grows
And there in a wood a Piggy-wig stood
  With a ring at the end of his nose,
    His nose,
    His nose,
  With a ring at the end of his nose.

"Dear Pig, are you willing to sell for one shilling
    Your ring?" Said the Piggy, "I will."
So they took it away, and were married next day
    By the Turkey who lives on the hill.
They dined on mince, and slices of quince,
    Which they ate with a runcible spoon;
And hand in hand, on the edge of the sand,
    They danced by the light of the moon,
            The moon,
            The moon,
They danced by the light of the moon.

LOUIS ZUKOFSKY

Third Movement: *In Cat Minor*

147   Hard, hard the cat-world.
148   On the stream of Vicissitude
149   Our milk flows lewd.

150   We'll cry, we'll cry,
151   We'll cry the more
152   And wet the floor,

153   Megrow, megrow,
154   Around around
155   The only sound

156   The prowl, our prowl,
157   Of gentlemen cats
158   With paws like spats

159   Who weep the nights
160   Till the nights are gone—
161   —And r-r-run—the Sun!

Tame Cat

It rests me to be among beautiful women
Why should one always lie about such matters?

I repeat:
It rests me to converse with beautiful women
Even though we talk nothing but nonsense,

The purring of the invisible antennae
Is both stimulating and delightful.

CHARLES BAUDELAIRE

The Cat (xxxvi)

Come, beautiful creature, sheathe your claws;
      Rest on my amorous heart,
And let me plunge in your marvellous eyes,
      Of mingled metal and agate.

When my fingers caress at leisure
      Your supple, elastic back,
And my hand tingles with pleasure
      From your body's electric contact,

I seem to see my mistress. Her regard,
      Like yours, nice animal,
Deep and cold, cuts and thrusts like a sword,
      And from her feet to her head's dark coronal,
A subtile air, a dangerous perfume,
      Swim round her brown body's dusky bloom.

(translated from the French by Doreen Bell)

PATRIZIA CAVALLI

You want me to be like one of your cats
castrated and parallel: they sleep in a row, as you
        know,
and are only cats offstage
when you don't see them. But I'll never be
castrated and parallel. I may leave,
but if I do it'll be sideways and in one piece.

(translated from the Italian by Gini Alhadeff)

LAWRENCE FERLINGHETTI

The Cat

    The cat
          licks its paw and
lies down in
         the bookshelf nook
                   She
        can lie in a
            sphinx position
   without moving for so
             many hours
and then turn her head
         to me and
            rise and stretch
  and turn
       her back to me and
      lick her paw again as if
           no real time had passed
     It hasn't
         and she is the sphinx with
       all the time in the world
           in the desert of her time
   The cat
     knows where flies die
        sees ghosts in motes of air
          and shadows in sunbeams

She hears
        the music of the spheres and
    the hum in the wires of houses
            and the hum of the universe
    in interstellar spaces
                    but
        prefers domestic places
                and the hum of the heater

The Young Cat and the Chrysanthemums

You mince, you start
advancing indirectly—
your tail upright
knocking about among the
frail, heavily flowered
sprays.

Yes, you are lovely
with your ingratiating
manners, sleek sides and
small white paws but
I wish you had not come
here.

RAINER MARIA RILKE

Black Cat

Glances even at an apparition
still seem somehow to reverberate;
here on this black fell, though, the emission
of your strongest gaze will dissipate:

as a maniac, precipitated
into the surrounding black, will be
halted headlong and evaporated
by his padded cell's absorbency.

All the glances she was ever swept with
on herself she seems to be concealing,
where, with lowering and peevish mind, they're
being downlooked upon by her and slept with.
As if wakened, though, she turns her face
full upon your own quite suddenly,
and in the yellow amber of those sealing
eyes of hers you unexpectedly
meet the glance you've given her, enshrined there
like an insect of some vanished race.

(translated from the German by J. B. Leishman)

MURIEL SPARK

Bluebell Among the Sables

The visitor came clothed with sables,
My dark and social friend.
The afternoon prospered after its kind
But they bore me, those intimate parliaments,
Those tea-times wear my heart away.

So I took half my pleasure in the sables
That flowed across her arm, the chair, the floor,
Sleek and fathomless like contemplative,
Living animals, the deep elect,
In ceremonious most limp obedience.

But the dark skins did not move, she felt them
      creep:
'My God! My sables!'
Indeed they were alive with a new life,
The sombre swiftly shot with quick and silver
Fur within fur. It was Bluebell, my beautiful,
My small and little cat pounding the sables.
Flat on her spine she tumbled them,
Shaking their kindly tails between her teeth.

'My furs! Your cat!'
I said, 'No need for alarm;
Those dead pelts can't cause Bluebell any harm.'
Pour soul, this put her in the wrong;
As one who somehow fails the higher vision,
She was meek: 'They cost the earth, my furs.'
I stroked the comical creature, she the sables,
And all came even.

For she said there was no damage, no damage.
It may be she had profit of the event;
As for myself that moment was well spent
When I saw Bluebell pummelling the sables.
I have the image, the gratuitous image
Miserly seized: of sable wonders glowing,
An order of the profound earth, of roots
And minerals evolved in civil strands,
Defined in which, the sprite, like air and like
A dawn asperges, green-eyed Bluebell plying
The sensuous fabric with her shining pads.

EUGENIO MONTALE

On a Stray Cat

The poor little stray
had not yet turned wild even though
thrown out from the block of flats
for fear he might tear the carpet with his claws.
I still remember him as I pass through the street
which saw events worthy of history
but not worth remembering. Perhaps
some crumb might fly of its own accord.

(translated from the Italian by G. Singh)

The Galloping Cat

Oh I am a cat that likes to
Gallop about doing good
So
One day when I was
Galloping about doing good, I saw
A Figure in the path; I said:
Get off! (Because
I am a cat that likes to
Gallop about doing good)
But he did not move, instead
He raised his hand as if
To land me a cuff
So I made to dodge so as to
Prevent him bringing it off,
Un-for-tune-ately
I slid
On a banana skin
Some Ass had left instead
Of putting in the bin. So
His hand caught me on the cheek
I tried
To lay his arm open from wrist to elbow
With my sharp teeth
Because I am

A cat that likes to gallop about doing good.
Would you believe it?
He wasn't there
My teeth met nothing but air,
But a Voice said: Poor Cat
(Meaning me) and a soft stroke
Came on me head
Since when
I have been bald
I regard myself as
A martyr to doing good.
Also I heard a swoosh,
As of wings, and saw
A halo shining at the height of
Mrs Gubbins's backyard fence,
So I thought: What's the good
Of galloping about doing good
When angels stand in the path
And do not do as they should
Such as having an arm to be bitten off
All the same I
Intend to go on being
A cat that likes to
Gallop about doing good

So
Now with my bald head I go,
Chopping the untidy flowers down, to
and fro,
An' scooping up the grass to show
Underneath
The cinder path of wrath
Ha ha ha ha, ho,
Angels aren't the only ones who do
not know
What's what and that
Galloping about doing good
Is a full-time job
That needs
An experienced eye of earthly
Sharpness, worth I dare say
(If you'll forgive a personal note)
A good deal more
Than all that skyey stuff
Of angels that make so bold as
To pity a cat like me that
Gallops about doing good.

CHRISTOPHER SMART

from *Jubilate Agno*

For I will consider my Cat Jeoffry.
For he is the servant of the Living God duly and
    daily serving him.
For at the first glance of the glory of God in the East
    he worships in his way.
For is this done by wreathing his body seven times
    round with elegant quickness.
For then he leaps up to catch the musk, which is the
    blessing of God upon his prayer.
For he rolls upon prank to work it in.
For having done duty and received blessing he
    begins to consider himself.
For this he performs in ten degrees.
For First he looks upon his fore-paws to see if they
    are clean.
For Secondly he kicks up behind to clear away
    there.
For Thirdly he works it upon stretch with the fore-
    paws extended.
For Fourthly he sharpens his paws by wood.
For Fifthly he washes himself.
For Sixthly he rolls upon wash.
For Seventhly he fleas himself, that he may not be
    interrupted upon the beat.

For Eighthly he rubs himself against a post.

For Ninthly he looks up for his instructions.

For Tenthly he goes in quest of food.

For having considered God and himself he will
consider his neighbor.

For if he meets another cat he will kiss her in
kindness.

For when he takes his prey he plays with it to give it
chance.

For one mouse in seven escapes by his dallying.

For when his day's work is done his business more
properly begins.

For he keeps the Lord's watch in the night against
the adversary.

For he counteracts the powers of darkness by his
electrical skin and glaring eyes.

For he counteracts the Devil, who is death, by
brisking about the life.

For in his morning orisons he loves the sun and the
sun loves him.

For he is of the tribe of Tiger.

For the Cherub Cat is a term of the Angel Tiger.

For he has the subtlety and hissing of a serpent,
which in goodness he suppresses.

For he will not do destruction, if he is well-fed,
neither will he splt without provocation.
For he purrs in thankfulness, when God tells him
he's a good Cat.
For he is an instrument for the children to learn
benevolence upon.
For every house is incomplete without him and a
blessing is lacking in the spirit.
For the Lord commanded Moses concerning the
cats at the departure of the Children of Israel
from Egypt.
For every family had one cat at least in the bag.
For the English Cats are the best in Europe.
For he is the cleanest in the use of his fore-paws of
any quadruped.
For the dexterity of his defense is an instance of the
love of God to him exceedingly.
For he is the quickest to his mark of any creature.
For he is tenacious of his point.
For he is a mixture of gravity and waggery.
For he knows that God is his Savior.
For there is nothing sweeter than his peace when
at rest.

For there is nothing brisker than his life when in
      motion.

For he is of the Lord's poor and so indeed is he
      called by benevolence perpetually—Poor
      Jeoffry! poor Jeoffry! the rat has bit thy throat.

For I bless the name of the Lord Jesus that Jeoffry is
      better.

For the divine spirit comes about his body to
      sustain it in complete cat.

For his tongue is exceeding pure so that it has in
      purity what it wants in music.

For he is docile and can learn certain things.

For he can set up with gravity which is patience
      upon approbation.

For he can fetch and carry, which is patience in
      employment.

For he can jump over a stick which is patience upon
      proof positive.

For he can spraggle upon waggle at the word of
      command.

For he can jump from an eminence into his master's
      bosom.

For he can catch the cork and toss it again.

For he is hated by the hypocrite and miser.

For the former is afraid of detection.

For the latter refuses the charge.

For he camels his back to bear the first notion of
business.

For he is good to think on, if a man would express
himself neatly,

For he made a great figure in Egypt for his signal
services.

For he killed the Ichneumon-rat very pernicious by
land.

For his ears are so acute that they sting again.

For from this proceeds the passing quickness of his
attention.

For by stroking of him I have found out electricity.

For I perceived God's light about him both wax and
fire.

For the Electrical fire is the spiritual substance,
which God sends from heaven to sustain the
bodies both of man and beast.

For God has blessed him in the variety of his
movements.

For, though he cannot fly, he is an excellent
clamberer.

For his motions upon the face of the earth are more
than any other quadruped.
For he can tread to all the measures upon the music.
For he can swim for life.
For he can creep.

ROBERTO BOLANO

No one sends you letters now
                             Under the lighthouse
at dusk   Lips parted by wind
They're making a revolution to the East   A cat
sleeps in your arms
Sometimes you're incredibly happy

(translated from the Spanish by Laura Healy)

You Know How a Cat

will bring a mouse it has
caught and lay it at your

feet so each morning I
bring you the poem that

I've written when I woke
up in the night as my tribute

to your beauty &
a promise of my love.

KAWAI CHIGETSU-NI

Propriety

Cats making love in the temple
But people would blame
A man and a wife for mating in such a place.

(translated from the Japanese by Kenneth Rexroth
and Ikuko Atsumi)

JEAN JOUBERT

Ancient Cat

Cat
old as this village
old as roots

each morning your eyes
(one of them veiled)
are larger.

What do you see in the haze
between rock and
cypress?
        These days you lie
stretched on my chest
to maintain your vigil.

My blood
pleases you, your claws
read me.

On your scrawny spine I place
this hand
        which knows and
wants not to know.

(translated from the French by Denise Levertov)

EZRA POUND

Mediterranean March
Black cat on the quince branch
mousing blossoms

AMY LOWELL

from "Chopin"

The cat and I
Together in the sultry night
Waited.
He greatly desired a mouse ;
I, an idea.
Neither ambition was gratified.
So we watched
In a stiff and painful expectation.
Little breezes pattered among the trees,
And thin stars ticked at us
Faintly,
Exhausted pulses
Squeezing through mist.

Those others, I said!
And my mind rang hollow as I tapped it
Winky, I said,
Do all other cats catch their mice?

Cat Asks Mouse Out
But then Neither is This

Mrs Mouse
Come out of your house
It is a fine sunny day
And I am waiting to play.

Bring the little mice too
And we can run to and fro.

FRANZ KAFKA

Little Fable

"Oh," said the mouse, "the world gets narrower with each passing day. It used to be so wide that I was terrified, and I ran on and felt happy when at last I could see walls in the distance to either side of me—but these long walls are converging so quickly that already I'm in the last room and there in the corner is the trap I'm running into." "You only have to change your direction," said the cat, and ate it up.

(translated from the German by Michael Hofmann)

The Innocent

The cat has his sport
and the mouse suffers
but the cat
      is innocent
  having no image of pain in him

     an angel
     dancing with his prey

carries it, frees it, leaps again
with joy upon his darling plaything

    a dance, a prayer!
How cruel the cat is to our guilty eyes

BASIL BUNTING

from "The Pious Cat"

By Heaven's decree there was a cat
in Haltwhistle, rough, rich and fat.
His fur was like a coat of mail
with lion's claws and leopard's tail.
When he went out and wailed at night
he made policemen shake with fright.
When he crouched in a flowerbed
big game hunters turned pale with dread.
All creatures beside him seemed tame.
Tibbald was this hero's name.

One day he visited the cellar
to scout for mice. Behind a pillar
he lay in ambush like a bandit
and it fell out as he had planned it -
a mouse crept from a crack and squeaked,
then leapt on a cask of beer (that leaked)
to drink, and shortly drank again.
Beer made him truculent and vain.
He snapped his fingers. 'Where's the cat?
I'll make his skin into a doormat.
I'll teach him: I'll give him what-for.
Cats? One good mouse can lick a score!

Tibbald! Who's he? Let him sneer and purr,
he'll cringe to me. The cat's a cur!'

Tibbald kept mum, but in the pause
you could hear him sharpening his teeth and claws.
When they were keen he made one jump
and caught the drunken mouse by the rump.

Mouse said: 'Please mister, let me off!
I did not mean to boast and scoff.
What I said was in liquor,
and tipsy tongues talk ten times quicker
than sober sense. Don't bear a grudge!'
but Tibbald only answered: 'Fudge!
Bring your remarks to a fullstop,'
then ate him and lapped the gravy up.

(adapted from the Persian of Obaid-e Zakani)

JUNG TZU

My Dressing Mirror Is a Humpbacked Cat

My dressing mirror is a humpbacked cat.
Continuously my image changes
As though on flowing water.
A humpbacked cat. A speechless cat.
A lonely cat. My dressing mirror.
A staring, round, startled eye.
A never waking dream wavers inside it.
Time? Radiance? Sorrow?
My dressing mirror is a cat of Fate.
Like a controlling face that locks up
My rich beauty in its own monotony,
My quiet virtue in its coarseness.
Steps, gestures, indolent as a long summer,
Desert its melodic steps,
Immured here in my dressing mirror—
A squatting cat.
A cat. A confused dream.
No light. No shadow.
Never once the reflection
Of my true image.

(translated from the Chinese by Kenneth Rexroth)

EDWIN BROCK

Hurry Up Please Its Time

Pussy cat, pussy cat
I know London was there
for carved like a mouse
in a kitchen chair
I heard my father
across the water speak
of dogs in Club Row
whitewashed to keep
their spots from showing

Cat, my father knew London
like the back of a hand
in a backstreet pub
turned over to sell
the cracks of the Union Canal

I do not think he'd ever seen
St. Paul's, The Tower or
the Queen, and the Guards
could change to red-eyed
stoats before he'd cross
a bridge to look

He left in a stinging fog
carrying pincers and pliers
to twist together
the tattered ends
of all the City's wires,
but his goodbye was longer
than he thought and even now
we have not caught up

Cat, do you remember
when we had a King
with a Jubilee and ate tea
in the streets and ran races
and scrambled for pennies?

Do you remember when Sunday was a noise of bells
and a one-armed rag-and-bone man
sang the same song
from Aldgate to the Old Kent Road?
What has happened since then?

His bones are on a London hill
built over by a block of flats
and that square mile
is the concrete cell
where I sat to sew bread and water

Cat, why can't God afford to live
in these churches any more?
Why does the Queen get older
all the time? Pussy cat
where have you been?
I have a mouse still waiting
to hide and a childhood
dying of nursery rhymes.

KIM HYESOON

I'll Call Those Things My Cats

They're alive: I'll talk about my invisible cats.
  They're alive. They lay two eggs every day.
  If they don't, they won't be able to multiply.
  After spring-cleaning, they're in danger of
  extinction. They disperse with a single puff.
  Yet, the cats are always alive in every corner.

They're very tiny: I don't need to give them anything
  to eat. Because I who am visible always leave
  flakes of my dead skin for them. Because my
  cats are tiny enough to build an apartment
  inside a single flake of dead skin.

They barely survive: They fall off when brushed
  off, they get eaten when sucked up, they put
  down their tails at the smallest cough. My
  cats are so tiny that when they are placed
  under a microscope and magnified 500,
  1000 times you can barely see their adorable
  moving lips. There's one that is fairly big. It's
  floating in air but always at the fringes of the
  dust. It trembles, afraid it might get blown
  away when I let out my breath, even afraid to
  be touched by a feather. They are powerless

against the cold. In summer, I can't even open the doors. They barely survive. Poor things. Please call me mother of cats. They're so tiny that I won't be able to embrace them. It can't be helped. I need to stow them in my pores at least. A red cat peeks out between the lines of a book. Such a cute thing. The cats are everywhere. They are in the center of my brain cells. Two eggs per day. Two eggs under a blanket. Red eyes, sweet cries. My cats that wiggle behind the sofa. When I return from school, they cover themselves with a blanket of dust on top of the closet—the sound of them purring, crying.

However: These adorable things. When my life gives out, they'd eat me up in a second. When it rains, they make me drag a leather sofa outdoors. They even build houses inside my nostrils. They'd even devour my elephant. They are like the stars that can't be seen in daylight.

(translated from the Korean by Don Mee Choi)

The Cat and the Moon

The cat went here and there
And the moon spun round like a top,
And the nearest kin of the moon,
The creeping cat, looked up.
Black Minnaloushe stared at the moon,
For, wander and wail as he would,
The pure cold light in the sky
Troubled his animal blood.
Minnaloushe runs in the grass
Lifting his delicate feet.
Do you dance, Minnaloushe, do you dance?
When two close kindred meet,
What better than call a dance?
Maybe the moon may learn,
Tired of that courtly fashion,
A new dance turn.
Minnaloushe creeps through the grass
From moonlit place to place,
The sacred moon overhead
Has taken a new phase.
Does Minnaloushe know that his pupils
Will pass from change to change,
And that from round to crescent,
From crescent to round they range?

Minnaloushe creeps through the grass
Alone, important and wise,
And lifts to the changing moon
His changing eyes.

HANS FAVEREY

The muffled thud with which the strange cat
lands in the room, and wakes me.
While she carries on sleeping

I look at the cat. This cat knows
I'm seeing it. The same moonless
night that on Hadrian's Wall

a snowy owl is sitting, motionless:
until the cat suddenly begins
to lick itself all over and I must have
shifted position. Are you awake?
(Shssst.) Go away cat.

(translated from the Dutch by Francis R. Jones)

Mujer

Oh, black Persian cat!
Was not your life
already cursed with offspring?
We took you for rest to that old
Yankee farm,—so lonely
and with so many field mice
in the long grass—
and you return to us
in this condition—!

Oh, black Persian cat.

ROBERT SOUTHEY

To a College Cat

Toll on, toll on, old Bell! I'll neither pray
Nor sleep away the hour. The fire burns bright,
And, bless the maker of this great-arm'd chair,
This is the throne of comfort! I will sit
And study most devoutly: not my Euclid,
For God forbid that I should discompose
That spider's excellent geometry!
I'll study thee, Puss: not to make a picture—
I hate your canvas cats and dog and fools,
Themes that pollute the pencil! let me see
The Patriot's actions start again to life,
And I will bless the artist who awakes
The throb of emulation. Thou shalt give,
A better lesson Puss! come look at me.
Lift up thine emerald eyes! aye, purr away,
For I am praising thee, I tell thee, Puss,
And Cats as well as Kings love flattery.
For three whole days I heard an old Fur Gown
Beprais'd, that made a Duke a Chancellor:
Trust me, though I can sing most pleasantly
Upon thy well-streak'd coat, to that said Fur
I was not guilty of a single rhyme!
'Twas an old turncoat Fur, that would sit easy

And wrap round any man, so it were tied
With a blue riband.
                What a magic lies
In beauty! thou on this forbidden ground
Mayest range, and when the Fellow looks at thee
Straight he forgets the statute. Swell thy tail
And stretch thy claws, most Democratic beast,
I like thine independence! Treat thee well,
Thou art as playful as young Innocence;
But if we play the Governor, and break
The social compact, God has given thee claws,
And thou hast sense to use them. Oh! that Man
Would copy this thy wisdom! spaniel fool,
He crouches down and licks his tyrant's hand
And courts oppression. Wiser animal,
I gaze on thee, familiar not enslaved,
And thinking how affection's gentle hand
Leads by a hair the large limb'd Elephant,
With mingled pity and contempt behold
His drivers goad the patient biped beast.

KAZUKO SHIRAISHI

Seven Happy Cats

seven cats are happy
always together with poet and wife
from east to west
coming over from that side to this
they got shots from doctors
they got names, identity cards, passports and visas
they arrived safely, all right

no matter who lives next door
the seven cats are happy
always together with poet and wife

who is the poet's mother?
where is her grave?
why did they come to live on this side?

no one needs to know the reason
the tight lipped poet says nothing
his kind wife is a fine cook

the seven cats were happy
ten years passed
three died last year of old age

three died last year
nothing could stop it

who is the poet's mother?
where is her grave?
that's why they came to live on this side

this is a great place
the tight-lipped poet speaks for the first time
"my wife really is a fine cook"

(translated from the Japanese by John Solt)

WILLIAM COWPER

from "The Retired Cat"

A Poet's cat, sedate and grave
As poet well could wish to have
Was much addicted to inquire
For nooks to which she might retire,
And where, secure as mouse in chink,
She might repose, or sit and think.

JOSÉ GARCIA VILLA

A,cat,having,attained,ninehood,
Shall,fear,ninthhood!
A,rule,to,prove,catness,

Or,negation,of,cathood.

Catness,cats,and,nineness,proves.
Ninthless,cats,prove,
Immortal,cats.

Wherefore,ninthhood,is,

Is,to,be,feared,
This,step,to,Ten!
So,cats,also,count,Ten.

NICANOR PARRA

Pussykatten

This cat is getting old

Several months back
Even his shadow looked
Like a spirit to him.

His electric whiskers
                        detected everything :
Beetle,
        housefly,
                    dragonfly,
Each had its own value.

Nowadays he spends his time
Snuggled up close to the brazier.

When the dog sniffs at him
Or rats nip at his tail
He doesn't even care.

The world goes past his half-shut eyes
Without stirring his interest.

Wisdom?
        mysticism?
                nirvana?
Surely all three
But mostly
        timefritteredaway.

White with ashes his spine
Shows he's a cat
Whose place is beyond good or evil.

(translated from the Spanish by Hardie St. Martin)

THOMAS GRAY

Ode on the Death of a Favourite Cat
Drowned in a Tub of Goldfishes

'Twas on a lofty vase's side,
Where China's gayest art had dyed
The azure flowers that blow;
Demurest of the tabby kind,
The pensive Selima, reclined,
Gazed on the lake below.

Her conscious tail her joy declared;
The fair round face, the snowy beard,
The velvet of her paws,
Her coat, that with the tortoise vies,
Her ears of jet, and emerald eyes,
She saw; and purred applause.

Still had she gazed; but 'midst the tide
Two angel forms were seen to glide,
The genii of the stream;
Their scaly armour's Tyrian hue
Through richest purple to the view
Betrayed a golden gleam.

The hapless nymph with wonder saw;
A whisker first and then a claw,
With many an ardent wish,
She stretched in vain to reach the prize.
What female heart can gold despise?
What cat's averse to fish?

Presumptuous maid! with looks intent
Again she stretch'd, again she bent,
Nor knew the gulf between.
(Malignant Fate sat by, and smiled)
The slippery verge her feet beguiled,
She tumbled headlong in.

Eight times emerging from the flood
She mewed to every watery god,
Some speedy aid to send.
No dolphin came, no Nereid stirred;
Nor cruel Tom, nor Susan heard;
A Favourite has no friend!

From hence, ye beauties, undeceived,
Know, one false step is ne'er retrieved,
And be with caution bold.
Not all that tempts your wandering eyes
And heedless hearts, is lawful prize;
Nor all that glisters, gold.

STEVIE SMITH

My Cats
a Witch speaks

I like to toss him up and down
A heavy cat weighs half a Crown
With a hey do diddle my cat Brown.

I like to pinch him on the sly
When nobody is passing by
With a hey do diddle my cat Fry.

I like to ruffle up his pride
And watch him skip and turn aside
With a hey do diddle my cat Hyde.

Hey Brown and Fry and Hyde my cats
That sit on tombstone for your mats.

GUILLAUME APOLLINAIRE

The Cat

I want in my own home:
A wife of sound reason
A cat among the books
Friends in every season
Without which I cannot live.

(translated by Roger Shattuck)

Sources

Guillaume Apollinaire, "The Cat" from *The Selected Writings of Guillaume Apollinaire*, translated by Roger Shattuck. Copyright © by Librairie Gallimard. Translation copyright © 1971 by Roger Shattuck.

Charles Baudelaire, "The Cat (LIV)," "The Cat (XXXVI)," and "Cats (LXIX)," from *The Flowers of Evil*, edited by Marthiel and Jackson Matthews. "The Cat (LIV)" translation copyright © 1989 by Roy Campbell. "The Cat (XXXVI)" translation copyright © 1989 by Doreen Bell. "Cats (LXIX)" translation copyright © 1989 by Anthony Hecht.

Elizabeth Bishop, "Lullaby for the Cat" from *The Complete Poems 1927–1979*. Copyright © 1979 by Elizabeth Bishop. Reprinted by permission of Farrar, Straus, and Giroux, Macmillian.

Roberto Bolaño, "No one sends you letters now ..." from *The Unknown University*. Copyright © 2007 by the Heirs of Roberto Bolaño. Translation copyright © 2013 by Laura Healy.

Edwin Brock, "Hurry Up Please Its Time" from *The Blocked Heart*. Copyright © 1976 by Edwin Brock.

Basil Bunting, "The Pious Cat" from *Complete Poems*. Copyright © 2000 by Basil Bunting.

Patrizia Cavalli, "You want me to be like one of your cats ..." from *My Poems Won't Change the World: Selected Poems*, edited by Gini Alhadeff. Copyright © 2014 by Patrizia Cavalli. Translation copyright © 2014 by Gini Alhadeff. Reprinted by permission of Farrar, Straus, and Giroux, Macmillan.

James Laughlin, "The Kenner's Cat" and "You Know How a Cat" from
  The Collected Poems of James Laughlin, edited by Peter
  Glassgold. Copyright © 1997 by James Lauglin.

Denise Levertov, "The Cat as Cat" from The Sorrow Dance.
  Copyright © 1966 by Denise Levertov. "The Innocent" from
  Collected Earlier Poems: 1940–1960. Copyright © 1979 by
  Denise Levertov.

Eugenio Montale, "On a Stray Cat" from *It Depends: A Poet's
  Notebook*. Copyright © 1977 by Arnoldo Mondadori Editore.
  Translation copyright © 1980 by G. Singh.

Nicanor Parra, "Pussykatten" from *Antipoems: New and Selected*,
  edited by David Unger. Copyright © 1985 by Nicanor Parra.

Fernando Pessoa, "Magnificat," translated by Margaret Jull Costa.
  Translation copyright © 2018 by Margaret Jull Costa.

Ezra Pound, "Tame Cat" from *Lustra of Ezra Pound*. "Mediterranean
  March" was sent in a letter to Katue Kitasono, dated March
  25, 1941, and printed in *Ezra Pound and Japan* by Sanehide
  Kodama; reprinted with permission of the estate of Ezra
  Pound.

Kenneth Rexroth, "Cat" from *Selected Poems*, edited by Bradford
  Morrow. Copyright © 1984 by Kenneth Rexroth.

Rainer Maria Rilke, "Black Cat" from *New Poems*, translated by J. B.
  Leishman. Translation copyright © 1964 by Hogarth Press.

Kazuko Shiraishi, "Seven Happy Cats" from *New Directions in Prose
  and Poetry 55*, edited by James Laughlin. Copyright © 1991
  by New Directions Publishing Company.

Stevie Smith, "Cat Asks Mouse Out," "Friskers" "The Galloping Cat,"
  "The Hound Puss," "My Cat Major," and "My Cats" from *All
  the Poems*, edited by Will May. Copyright © 1972 by Stevie
  Smith.